The *"Saved by the Belle"* eBook Series

I0510273

# THE NINETY DAY REALTOR
*FOR THE NEW AND ASPIRING REAL ESTATE PROFESSIONAL*

Written By

Ayanna Chanel Fultz
*"The Southern Belle of Real Estate"*

# PREFACE

Unknowingly, real estate has always been in my heart. At an
early age, I took an avid interest in home layout and design,
historic architecture, and community development. Being a
native New Orleanian, every Summer during early
childhood, my Mother would plan a week of activities for me
to enjoy which included visits to local museums and historic
neighborhoods: the Children's Museum, the Wax Museum,
the New Orleans Museum of Art, the historic Treme
neighborhood, and the Garden District, just to name a few.
Riding on the streetcar during our daily adventures, I felt
magic brewing in my spirit as my young eyes eagerly gazed
upon the large, luxurious homes that lined St. Charles
Avenue. After arriving home from our daily journeys, I would
hurry to my room to begin using my writing utensils and
paper to draw what I saw that day. Often times, those

pictures were filled with my vision of beautiful homes accompanied by gorgeously sprawling landscapes; each home possessing some unique quality that set it apart from the next.

It's safe to say that I've always been a "visionary"; whether it was orchestrating imaginary events and programs during family get-togethers in my Grandmother's living room or always being selected to choreograph and lead dance routines in school. When boredom struck, I transcribed plans to establish a small shopping mall for teenagers to "stay out of trouble" as I'd say. Plans included a bowling alley, a skating rink, and a tutoring center. The establishment had one special purpose; to aid in the growth of the community and to enhance the lives of budding youth. The tutoring center was the closest to my heart. I remember my grandma always telling me,"You have to get your lesson first," whenever I wanted to go and play with my friends before completing my homework. Like most kids, I enjoyed spending time with my friends but nothing satisfied my heart more than sketching and "perfecting" my dream home. My sketches included a large office, a movie theatre, and a revolving closet, an idea I acquired from "Cher," the main character from "Clueless", my favorite movie at the time.

Looking back, what is most ironic about this time in my life was that no adult took note of my interest in real estate. Of course, I don't fault them 20+ years later; especially since I've always had very involved and attentive parents. However, I do want to emphasize to whomever this publication may encounter: pay attention to the activities that excite your children. If your children can entertain themselves for hours doing something without tire and with much enthusiasm, make note and begin to implement more activities to advance and cultivate that skillset. Help them get on the road to fulfilling their life's purpose without coercion.

My first ten years of adulthood were spent acquiring experience and degrees in a field I knew the entire time I had very little interest. I felt like I was in jail. I was good at it but I knew it wasn't my purpose; simply because it didn't look or feel like freedom. Why did I continue to pursue careers that did not satisfy me? It was largely because it sounded good, "Manager of…", "Director of…", " Executive Director of…", not because it was my passion. I realized that what sounds good does not equate to a happy and fulfilling life. Quality of life is so much more important than money acquired.

In my first 90 days as a Realtor, I have acquired so many jewels of wisdom from mentors including my Broker and fellow Realtors. I've made mistakes and faced a number of challenges but my fire still burns passionately bright for "my beloved real estate". I can say I am truly grateful for those who have come into my life and helped me to recall those innocent childhood memories and realize my life's purpose. I dedicate this publication to you. Let's get started!

# "WHY" REAL ESTATE?

As we begin every new venture in our lives, we should simply ask ourselves… "Why am I doing this?" WHY entrepreneurship? WHY should I pursue a graduate degree? WHY should I make this investment? But for the sake of this publication, "Why real estate?" Have you asked yourself that question? You'll hear many people's responses centered around money. Trust me, you can make loads of money in real estate, but I promise "money motivation", as I call it, will only carry you so far. There *will be* periods of time you'll go without generating any money and you will question if real estate is right for you. As Realtors, we work in sales, the sale of homes, and just like any traditional sales job, we are compensated via commission. Therefore, as one of my more seasoned realtor friends puts it, "We eat what we kill!" So, it's probably a good idea to have multiple "why's" because when times get tough and the funds in your bank account begin to dwindle, your interest in money alone will *not* sustain you.

A perfect parallel I can draw here is my personal struggle with weight loss and maintaining a healthy lifestyle. My entire life I have struggled with my weight. I have always been one of the heaviest students in class during my school years and of course I endured much emotional trauma and mental anguish because of it. In high school, I remember starving myself and only eating Nutri-Grain bars in hopes that I'd drop the pounds. Many times, I'd exercise to near exhaustion thinking that I'd begin to melt the pounds quickly. By high school, weight loss became an obsession as I desired to wear the clothes that the smaller girls were wearing and receive male attention just like my friends. But it wasn't until the age of 19 when I experienced a major health scare that I knew a long-term, effective change had to occur. I'll never forget the doctor's words, "Type 2 Diabetes is avoidable but once you acquire it, it's something you'll deal with for the rest of your life." I was diagnosed pre-diabetic *and* pre-hypertensive. That scared me poop-less! I weighed a whopping 276 pounds; way too much for my 5'5" frame. I remember being constantly physically uncomfortable and I held a generally discontent view of life in general. After leaving the doctor's office, I was broken, upset, and as my Great Grandmother would put it "sick and tired of being sick and tired".

I decided, April 26, 2009, that I needed to do something about my sedentary lifestyle and eating habits. So, for the next 4-5 days, I entered a deep meditation period (what I now call the "get your mind right" stage of effective personal change) and I agreed that change was a necessity. I told myself, "Food will always be there." I also agreed that I would learn to like physical activity and would employ different exercise and dance forms to reach my weight loss goals. But as my goal start date of May 1st approached, I became increasingly apprehensive. I thought to myself: "What if I don't lose anything?"; "I don't know what I'm doing! Who am I kidding?!" But this is where I began to employ my "why". I calmed myself and pondered, "*Why* do I want to lose weight?" After heavy contemplation, I began to write:

> "*Because I'm tired of being teased.*"
> "*Because I want to live a long life.*"

*"Because I'm tired of buying expensive, plus size clothes."*

*"Because fat jokes really aren't funny. They're tacky."*

*"Because I don't want to die."*

*"Because I want to look and feel my best!"*

By the time I'd finished, I had written nearly 50 purpose-filled "why" statements. I knew that I needed multiple "why's" in order to keep me motivated for the journey ahead.

Well, real estate is quite similar. Every day will not be a good day. Every deal will not see the closing table. Every realtor will not be professional. Every client will not be easily pleased. So, how will you keep yourself motivated during those times? Determine *and* physically list your "why's" and you will surely meet your long and short term business goals.

# ONE STEP AT A TIME

In life, many times people underestimate the effects and power of a step. One step can easily change a life, circumstance, or environment and ultimately hones the power to alter outcomes. As a new realtor, I understand that each step bears its own significance and plays a major part in the client experience and solidifying a transaction. In order to become a Realtor, my first step was to apply to real estate school. Without that initial application, becoming a real estate agent would've continued to be one of my lifelong dreams; all because I refused to take that first step. Although it sounds simple enough, there are many people who fear just *one* step. It can be daunting to the fearful because that step takes effort and signifies progression... no matter how large or small.

Real estate is a lot to digest partly because it's ever-changing. A home may be on the market today and under contract tomorrow. (And that's no exaggeration.). Remember to allow yourself time to collect, analyze, and digest the new material. Between types of loans, different grant programs, and stipulations contained in the purchase agreement, your brain will quickly spin into a troubled frenzy. Just take a deep breath and take it a step at a time. No two deals are the same. Absolutely no deal is guaranteed. Even 2-week, all cash offers may fall through. (I know this first hand and it's *not* fun!) Just take it in stride. Dust yourself off. Learn from the experience and move on.

My friend and personal photographer, Jerome*, is the self proclaimed "King of Analogies" and the way he explains it is: Building a business is a process. It's very involved and tedious but what matters is the *"quality of effort"* you invest into each step along the way. It's like building a house. If you build with cheap materials and skip the implementation of needed steps, your finished product will be equally shiny and new as a premium quality built home. However, over time the property will begin to easily wear and crumble causing you to have to redo work and, if it's bad enough, tear down and rebuild. A house (your business) cannot effectively sustain itself on a weak, poorly constructed foundation. That's why it's up to you to ensure your business' success by laying a firm, sound, quality foundation… "one step at a time." Trust the process.

# WHAT SETS YOU APART?

When we think about real estate, we usually think about the classic, professional headshot of a man or woman in a dark suit with their arms folded over their chest coupled with that signature pseudo-confident, "Please pick me!" smile. But what *really* sets them apart from the next realtor? What makes potential clients want to entrust their financial future with them?

Before I began my real estate education course, I was told by a loan officer friend that every month in the state of Louisiana, approximately 60 new realtors enter into the industry but only 20-30% employ any type of real estate promotion and marketing. In addition to that, studies show that 75% of new agents fail within the first year. So, it's very important that you figure out "what sets you apart".

What personal and business qualities do you possess that may attract new buyer, seller, or investment clients? Basically, how do you plan to brand and market yourself and your services? I've seen realtors in speedos on billboards (Such an attention grabber, I know!). I've seen realtors record themselves participating in social media challenges, create funny videos in their listings, and the list goes on and on. But that's the fun thing about real estate; *you* determine the image you want to portray.

In life, I've found that authenticity wins every time and that goes for real estate as well. Being authentic and arriving at a place of internal contentment not only puts *us* at ease but also those interacting with us, no matter the platform. People subconsciously appreciate an authentic disposition. Anything less puts them on edge. You'll find the only naysayers you'll have are those who are projecting their insecurities onto you. So, don't be afraid to be *unique*. Establish your presence in your market and have fun. The clientele will come and based on clientele quality and analytical feedback, adjust accordingly.

As you may have guessed by now, marketing is very important in the field of real estate and it's important that you employ *multiple* marketing techniques that are effective. As my Broker says, "When they think of real estate, they should immediately think of you!" Over the years, she has implemented stellar marketing techniques and is so graciously passing what she has learned to us, her team of "Rockstar Realtors."

Creating a marketing plan is the first step to discovering and streamlining "what sets you apart." The first question you should ask yourself is, "Who am I?" In other words, what do you represent? How do you want to make people feel when they interact with you? What makes you special? For me, it was easy deciding what makes me special.I have worn large derby hats and fascinators since I was 18 years of age, orchestrated a number of women's empowerment events (which required attendees to don dainty headpieces), and I'm almost always mistaken as a pastor's wife. So, I've been what can be thought of as a "Southern Belle" for some time now; therefore, adopting the title in relation to real estate meshed well with my existing image.

The internet has plenty websites that list some of the most successful real estate marketing techniques including lessons on how to attract subscribers to your mailing list, targeted social media engagement, and door hanger templates and disbursement techniques. There's even lead companies that "guarantee" clientele at a monthly fee.

Yes, there's plenty competition out there. There are many agents; both new and seasoned. But the most promising part is none of them are you and that, my friend, is your power. Capitalize on that! So, with that being said, as a brand new realtor, it's important that you quickly discover "what sets you apart".

## GUIDE TO AN EFFECTIVE MARKETING PLAN
## FOR THE NEW REAL ESTATE AGENT

About 80% of real estate centers around marketing and your quality, timing, and placement of such marketing. So, it's imperative that you complete a succinct marketing plan in order to reach your business goals. Simply put, if no one knows you are a Realtor, of course no one will know to patronize you. This is why marketing is extremely important.

Ideally, marketing plans should be completed at the beginning of the annual year or the start of your business' fiscal year. Yet, throughout the year, you're bound to make changes for different reasons that may come as a result of market fluctuations, client feedback, and follower/fan engagement. What's most important is that you stay ahead of the curve as it relates to marketing in your respective area. Implementing marketing schemes, words, phrases, or marketing materials that a competitor (in our case, another realtor) has already implemented will not fair out well for your brand. As emphasized previously in this book, *originality* and *authenticity* is key! These qualities keep your followers and potential clients engaged and helps to keep you on a different playing field than those in your particular market.

Use these 7 steps to assist in your real estate marketing success.

*STEP 1: Determine Your Angle*

How would you like to approach real estate? Do you want to be seen as earnest and ultra professional? Fun and interactive? Girly and confident? The key to this step is to capitalize on your authentic self. That'll be easier to maintain long-term.

*Step 2: Research. Scope out other realtor's marketing techniques.*

The internet and social media are powerful. These two avenues give you the ability to research anyone and anything. Use them! Discover who are the top performers in your area or maybe even at your brokerage. What techniques are they using to attract clients? What organizations are they a part of? Where do they hang out? Then, in contrast, identify what they are lacking. Here is where you are allowed to be critical. What don't they do? Are there any personality flaws? Just make note and include in your analysis. This will help you to further reinforce your angle and offer what they aren't.

*Step 3: Determine and list your business goals for your first 12 months in real estate.*
These goals should consist of both monetary and marketing goals as the two areas work in a complementary fashion.

*Step 4: Contemplate and then draw up a step by step plan to achieve each goal.*
This step closely resembles what I like to call a series of "mini marketing plans" within your general, large-scope marketing plan. During this step, it's important that you are realistic. I'll use weight loss again as an example:

GOAL: Lose 5 pounds by March 31, 2018.

- ❏ Drink at least 6- 8oz glasses of water a day.
- ❏ Exercise at least 4 days a week with a focus on strength training.
- ❏ Adopt a protein-rich, low-carb diet
- ❏ Dabble in intermittent fasting 3 days of the week
- ❏ Fast food/restaurant eating no more than 1 meal a week

- ❏ No mixed alcoholic beverages. Red wine permitted occasionally.
- ❏ No eating or snacking after 7pm; Drink water when "hunger" arises after that time.

*Step 5: Time your steps to each goal.*

Just like the above example, give yourself deadlines but know that your audience can only digest one thing at a time. Too much information at once will confuse and bombard them and will undoubtedly hurt your brand. Streamline your approach. Timing is everything.

*Step 6: Take action.*

It's time to get the show on the road! Implement your plans!

*Step 7: Monitor. Analyze. Re-strategize. Implement.*

You are not done yet! Now it's time to study your audience and their reactions. Don't talk *at* them. Engage them. Respond to them. Attend and sponsor events where you may have the opportunity to meet followers/supporters and generate new potential clients and allies. If things ever begin to get redundant or "boring", re-energize your marketing avenues by introducing something new or implementing a new engagement or involvement tactic. Feel free to get creative here.

# NO SALE!

As we mentioned previously, 75% of first year realtors quit and I can almost guarantee you it's because the majority of their first year was spent with "no sales". It's unfortunate but a definite reality. This also ties into what we spoke about during the first chapter of this publication, your "why". By this time your "why" may be, "*Why am I doing this again?*"

During your season of struggle and sacrifice, which usually runs concurrently with receiving no sales, you'll discover your "why" by force if you haven't done your due diligence to get your vision in order before this crucial time. Also during this time, is when a person's love or "divine hate" for real estate emerges. The "struggle" has a funny way of helping our true intentions emerge. The key is to take heed and pay attention to your interests and focus at this critical time. If you weather the storm, great! You are most likely in it for the long haul. If not, you may want to re-evaluate, regroup, and re-strategize; even if that means a career change. The sooner you discover your life's purpose and pursue it, the happier you shall be.

Two outstanding realtors at my brokerage both began their career with no sales their first year.  Although, they both admit their marketing techniques were nearly nonexistent during their initial year; which made it difficult for consumers to identify them as agents. I'm sure they got discouraged and wanted to throw up their hands and quit but their love for real estate and building a more promising future for themselves and their families (amongst other personal and business interests and goals) kept them going.

The moral of the story is: Don't let the possibility of no or just a few sales your first year discourage you. Keep going! Every sale won't go through. You will hit snags. You will lose clients. But that is ok. Just learn to ride the wave and know that better days are just on the horizon. Be encouraged.

# YOUR ATTITUDE DETERMINES YOUR ALTITUDE

There's nothing worse than a bad attitude. Don't you agree? Often, bad attitudes are accompanied by bad energy and can make for an overall bad experience. When we walk into a restaurant, we expect the employees to have a pleasantly accommodating attitude. When they don't, the entire experience begins to go downhill. Suddenly, you notice that the utensils are not clean. Your food is cold and you also notice that no one in the kitchen is wearing gloves or hairnets. "How disgusting!", you think. If you decide against requesting a refund, you make note to never return to the establishment again. Is that how you want your clients to feel? One of the biggest mistakes I've seen realtors make is treating clients (and even other realtors) poorly. The goal is to develop repeat, lifelong clients and for them to refer their contacts to you for more business. Whether a client is a buyer pre-approved for merely $100,000 or a property management client only paying you less than $100 per month for your services, *all* clients are to be treated like million-dollar clients because even the smallest of deals can somehow morph into multi-million dollar contracts and great references.

In the event a client is causing undue stress and hassle, before you become visibly upset, it's probably best to refer them to one of your trusted realtor colleagues who you may feel may mesh well with the client's personality, interests, and disposition.

During your journey in real estate, you'll encounter all types of realtors: the gimmick-y, fast talking realtor, the know-it-all realtor, the unprofessional/careless realtor, the snippy realtor, and the lazy realtor, just to name a few. But so far, my favorite just so happens to be the braggy realtor. They're undoubtedly fun to observe.

Years ago, at the very start of my career in healthcare, I joined a local civic organization to hopefully assist with my job search. Even while unemployed, I was surprisingly appointed twice to a pretty coveted board position. Because of my stature within the organization at the time, I was able to meet many other rising young professionals. One being a local realtor just beginning her journey with a nationwide brokerage. Her name was Jessica*. She dressed well and always wore her real estate name tag, but usually seemed pretty distant from the majority; even in networking and social situations. It wasn't a spirit of reservation or nervousness. It was a sort of condescending, judgmental heir. I kept thinking to myself, "How does she sell houses?" Well, ironically, I befriended her, as I do just about anyone I am around long enough due to my amicable demeanor. I began to mentally unpack her questionable disposition, giving her the benefit of the doubt.

Once we connected, she seemed to open up a bit more. Because of her "reserved" nature and my open social disposition, she often gravitated to my side, as if I were her link to solidifying more business within the organization, which was cool with me. I'm all about helping others further themselves. But there's one conversation I'll never forget; an exchange she had with another realtor. The other realtor was someone I'd personally introduced her to, as I was excited to connect them being as though they were in the same field. Their conversation was pretty uncomfortable as she seemed like she had no interest in connecting with him and only resorted to asking him his stats in regards to yearly sales and current listings. I don't believe he had a conversation with her again and I was pretty embarrassed that I had even initiated them meeting one another. That bridge was completely burned and there's nothing she could do to recover from it nor did it seem she felt anything was wrong with the exchange. Even at that point in time, I understood the theory of competition but more importantly, I also recognized the importance of allies within your career field. Little did she know, Kenneth* was a first year realtor that was experiencing uber success at the time due to his connections within the New Orleans Saints Football franchise. He was also such a giving, humble spirit who gave regularly to local charities.

After enjoying immense success in real estate, Kenneth* enrolled in law school and is now a rising litigation attorney in our nation's capital, Washington D.C.; forever elevating because of his big heart and humble spirit. I haven't a clue what *Jessica\** is doing. I don't think anyone knows or cares either.

Understand that energy is powerful and what you manifest into the universe will sprout up and sew itself into your life tenfold. Be mindful and stay balanced.

# PUT THE PEDAL TO THE METAL

After your first 90 days, you'll be ready to put the "pedal to the metal". You will have taken all the steps required to become a Realtor and gotten your feet wet by actually working with clients and getting familiar with real estate transactions. Although it will take a while to get comfortable with your new role, you have taken the first few steps to a prosperous real estate future.

Again, first you want to determine your "why" by digging deep and identifying your drive and inspiration to mentally and spiritually fuel your career in real estate. Then, you want to remember to take your real estate journey one step at a time building a quality foundation in order to support your future success. Next, determine what sets you apart. What makes you unique? Why should a prospective client use your services to assist in reaching their long and/or short term real estate goals? Then, you will need to accept the fact that you may go a long while without making a sale due to a wide variety of probable circumstances. Despite this, what's most important is that you stay focused and concentrate your energy on completing tasks and implementing plans that will prove beneficial in the long run. One of the most important steps is to approach every situation with a positive attitude, as this will ultimately determine your career sustainability and long-term success.

And lastly, once you have implemented all these steps to propel your business to the next level, you should be comfortable enough to "put the pedal to the metal"!

Be intentional. Be encouraged. Stay focused. 'Til next time.

# ABOUT THE AUTHOR

Branding herself as *"The Southern Belle of Real Estate"*, Louisiana Licensed Realtor Ayanna Chanel Fultz has taken a very unique approach to real estate in the Louisiana market.

After a 10 year career in Healthcare Administration and Transportation Logistics, "the Belle" decided to pursue her lifelong dream of becoming the *"South's Premier Realtor"*. Ms. Fultz is a graduate of St. Leo University in Tampa, Florida, where she attained a Master of Business Administration. She attended Jackson State University in Jackson, Mississippi, where she earned a Bachelor's degree in Healthcare Administration, Summa Cum Laude. Before her tenure at JSU, she attained an Associates degree in General Studies-Biology from Delgado Community College, where she earned the honor of Phi Theta Kappa International Honor Society graduate and she also achieved the honor of Valedictorian at her high school graduation from St. Mary's Academy in New Orleans, Louisiana.

She maintains membership in several social, civic, and religious organizations within the New Orleans community and is also the Founder, Visionary, and President of the all-female non-profit organization, the Paragon Society, founded in 2015 to reinstate class, refinement, and a dedicated and selfless service to the community through 5 service-driven signature initiatives including a leadership and development academy for young ladies entitled "Paragon Academy". Ayanna also holds great significance in Louisiana Carnival history as the very first African American Carnival Queen to reign in Jefferson Parish, Louisiana.

Writing and helping to uplift and inspire those around her has always been a great pastime for "the Belle" and she is happy to now share her love, thoughts, and wisdom on a worldwide stage.

---

# *Keep up with "The Belle"!*

### Facebook
"Sold By the Belle"

### Instagram
@soldbythebelle

### Web
www.soldbythebelle.com